ACROSS AMERICA

EXPEDITION

THE STORY OF LEWIS & CLARK

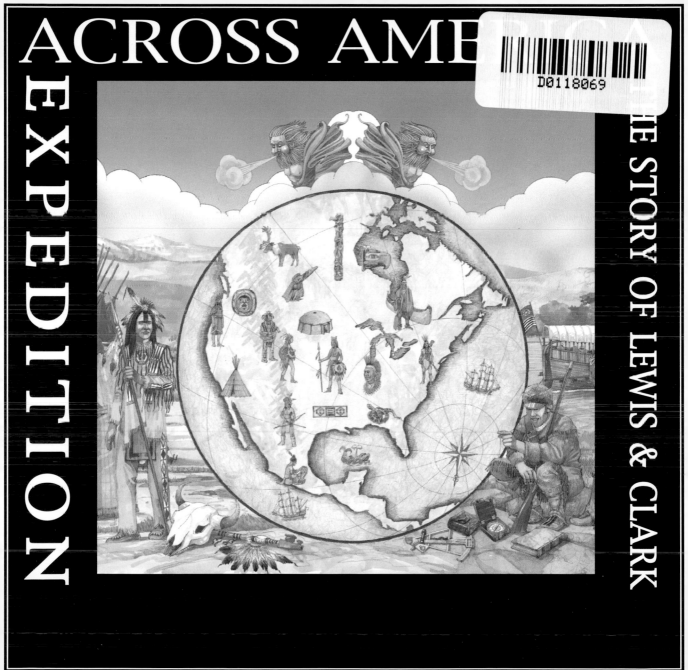

EDITOR APRIL McCROSKIE
An SBC Book, created, designed, and produced by
The Salariya Book Company
25 Marlborough Place
Brighton
East Sussex
BN1 1UB

© The Salariya Book Company Limited MCMXCVIII

Franklin Watts 1998
First American edition by
Franklin Watts
A Division of Grolier Publishing
90 Sherman Turnpike
Danbury, CT 06816

ISBN 0-531-14455-0 (lib.bdg.) 0-531-15342-8 (pbk.)

Visit Franklin Watts on the Internet at:
http:// publishing, grolier.com

Library of Congress Cataloging-in-Publication Data
Morley, Jacqueline
    Across America : the story of Lewis and Clark / written by
Jacqueline Morley : illustrated by David Antram : created and designed
by David Salariya. --1st American ed.
    p. cm -- (Expedition)
  Includes Index.
 Summary: Describes the Lewis and Clark Expedition Across America,
emphasizing the enormous adventure and technological challenges
encountred.
  ISBN 0-531-14455-0
 1. Lewis and Clark Expedition (1804-1806)--Juvenile literature. 2. West
(U.S.)--Discovery and exploration--Juvenile literature. 3. Lewis,
Meriwether 1774-1809--Juvenile literature. 4. Clark, William, 1770-1838--
Juvenile literature. [1. Lewis, Meriwether, 1774-1809. 2. Clark, William,
1770-1838. 3. Explorers. 4.Lewis and Clark Expedition (1804-1806) 5.
West (U.S.)--Discovery and exploration.] I. Antram, David, 1958- ill. II.
Salariya, David. III. Title. IV. Series.
F592.7.M676 1998
917.804'2--dc21   97034692   CIP/AC

JACQUELINE MORLEY
is a graduate of Somerville College, Oxford. She has
written historical fiction and non-fiction, having a
particular interest in the history of everyday life.
She is a major contributor to the popular Timelines
series, and has written *How would you survive in the
American West?*

DAVID ANTRAM
was born in Brighton in 1958. He studied at
Eastbourne College of Art and then worked in
advertising for fifteen years. He lives in Sussex
with his wife and two children.

DAVID SALARIYA
was born in Dundee, Scotland. He has designed and
created many new series of children's books. In 1989,
he established The Salariya Book Company Ltd.
He lives in Brighton with his wife, the illustrator
Shirley Willis, and their son Jonathan.

ACROSS AMERICA
The Story of Lewis & Clark

Written by JACQUELINE MORLEY

Illustrated by DAVID ANTRAM

Created and designed by
DAVID SALARIYA

W

FRANKLIN WATTS
A Division of Grolier Publishing
NEW YORK • LONDON • HONG KONG • SYDNEY
DANBURY, CONNECTICUT

CONTENTS

EXPEDITION

INTRODUCTION

IN 1783 the colonial lands in North America that belonged to Britain won their independence after a fierce war. The United States – the new country they formed – was then about a quarter of its present size, owning much of the eastern part of the continent as far as the Mississippi River. The rest, including a vast unexplored wilderness to the west, was claimed by European nations. If a way through that wilderness could be found, American traders would be able to travel across, capture the rich Pacific coast fur trade, and establish U.S. rights to the land. Then the American nation could expand across the continent, from the Atlantic Ocean in the east to the Pacific in the west.

This was the dream of America's third president, Thomas Jefferson. In 1803 Jefferson took practical steps towards making his dream come true. He sent an expedition to find a route across the vast continent. The men he chose to lead the expedition were Meriwether Lewis and William Clark. This book tells the story of the hardship faced by these two brave explorers and their team.

c. 1800: The Spanish in North America
As well as Florida and the southwest, Spain owned Louisiana, a vast and almost totally unexplored region stretching from the Mississippi to the Rockies (Rocky Mountains). In 1800 it surrendered this area to France.

c. 1800: The British in North America
The British, in Canada, had the easiest access to the continent's most desired asset – furs. Traders went far into the wilds to buy beaver furs from the Native Americans, to sell to the Canadian fur companies.

JEFFERSON chose a young army officer, Captain Meriwether Lewis, to lead the expedition. Lewis's task was to follow the Missouri River to its source in the Rocky Mountains (mentioned vaguely in Native American accounts). Beyond the mountains lay the Columbia River. Lewis was to find its source and travel down the river to the ocean. The peoples he met on the way were to be told of the benefits of giving up war with each other and turning to trade with the Americans – not with the British.

Through the winter of 1802-1803 President Jefferson and Lewis pored over maps at Monticello, the President's home.

Spring 1803, Monticello
Lewis practiced taking astronomical measurements to help him work out directions. This was part of a course of studies that Jefferson devised.

April 1803, U.S. arsenal
How many guns and how much ammunition would the expedition need? Lewis had to get it right. *Inset above;* the latest rifle model, 1803.

May 1803, Philadelphia
To complete his training, Lewis visited Philadelphia to meet famous astronomers and geographers, and to buy scientific instruments.

•THE WAY TO THE WEST?•

c. 1800: The U.S. in North America
American ships were on the north Pacific coast, buying furs to sell at a profit in China. In 1792 a trader found the mouth of the Columbia River.

c. 1800: The French in North America
Napoleon, First Consul of France, was at war with Britain and found Louisiana too much to defend. He told his ministers to make a deal with the United States. France agreed to sell Louisiana to the U.S., to keep Britain out.

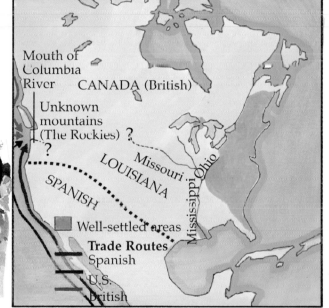

Saluting the acquisition of Louisiana in December, 1803. Now exploring the region was even more urgent.

May 1803, Philadelphia
Lewis talked to specialists in botany, zoology, and taxidermy, so that he would be able to note new species and preserve specimens.

July 1803, Pittsburgh
Lewis found that the keelboat he had ordered was still only half built. Its builder was drunken and uncooperative. This was a maddening delay.

August 1803, Louisville
Ready at last, Lewis sailed down the Ohio River to join William Clark, the trusted army colleague he had chosen as the expedition's co-leader.

May 1804: The Final Loading Up

From the start the expedition would be out of touch with all normal sources of supply. No one knew what lay ahead. The leaders had to gamble on having packed the right things, and enough of each.

Provisions

1 Rifles. 2 Writing tools. 3 Dried and salted rations. 4 Fishing tackle. 5 Axes. 6 Clothes. 7 Medicines. They also took tent cloth, mosquito netting, cooking pots, blacksmith's tools, and lead for making bullets.

CAPTAINS Lewis and Clark with a crew of fifteen, in the keelboat and two pirogues (open boats), reached the Mississippi in November 1803. Because of the boatbuilder's delay it was too late to start up the Missouri because it froze in winter.

The team spent the winter camped near St. Louis and trained for life in the wilderness. The captains had learned a lot already. The keelboat was proving awkward to handle, so they needed to take on more crew members. That meant buying more supplies and weapons.

The toughest volunteers were chosen and sworn in as soldiers for the trip.

Summer 1804

Northwest up the Missouri. Navigation upstream was troublesome. Fallen, half-submerged trees threatened to damage the boats.

The Keelboat

The heavy keelboat was hard to steer in the changing currents of the river. It often got stuck on sandbars and had to be hauled clear.

Mosquito Swarms

Mosquitoes got in the men's eyes, noses, ears, and throats. The only cure was smoke from the camp fire, or to coat themselves in grease.

• PROVISIONS FOR THE EXPEDITION •

Trade Goods

The expedition took goods such as glass beads, mirrors, blankets, needles, scissors, thread, knives, and trinkets of all kinds to trade with the Native Americans.

The captains now with a team of 45, including an interpreter, set off on May 18, 1804.

Were There Enough Trade Goods?

The expedition was relying on these trade goods to make friends and trade with people on the way. But Clark was worried. He thought the government had been mean with the funds to buy them.

Seaman

While Clark directed the boats, Lewis explored the riverbanks with his dog Seaman – an important member of the team.

Keeping a Record

Each night Lewis described everything he had seen that day – scenery, minerals, plants, and animals – in his journal for Jefferson.

On Guard

The team was armed and on its guard constantly. It believed the way to ensure that encounters were peaceful was to discourage attack.

August 3, 1804: The First Council

The Captains invited Oto chiefs to a meeting, to tell them that they had a new "Great Father" (Jefferson) who was American. Lewis made an hour-long speech explaining Jefferson's message of peace and trade.

August 3, 1804: A Presentation

The Otoes listened politely but seemed baffled. There was always war between tribes. How else could warriors win glory? But they accepted gifts and were presented with medals showing a picture of Jefferson's head.

Hunting parties went out regularly to get food.

THE EXPEDITION inched its way upriver, between lush prairies. On a good day it made around 18 miles (30 kilometers), but much less if strong currents prevented rowing and the team had to struggle with tow-lines along the riverbanks. By August it was entering a vast grassland (modern South Dakota), home to many tribes of Plains Indians. Here the captains had their first chance to deliver Jefferson's peace message. It got a mixed welcome, especially from the Sioux, who resented white traders.

Buffalo

Beaver

Elk

Coyote

Animals of the Plains

The area teemed with wildlife – beaver in the streams, elk and deer in woods by the river, and herds of buffalo on the plains.

August 12, 1804

A wolf-like animal new to everyone (a coyote) barked at the keelboat. Lewis wanted to shoot a specimen but the coyote got away.

August 23, 1804

The team shot a buffalo. The meat was delicious. Each person could eat over 8.8 pounds (4 kilograms) of meat after a day on the boats.

August 18, 1804: A Court Martial

After three months the strain of the trip was beginning to tell. One of the privates, Reed, tried to desert. After three days he was caught, tried, and sentenced to a lashing.

August 18, 1804: A Birthday

The day had a happier ending as it was Lewis's 30th birthday. The men were given extra whiskey to celebrate. They danced round the camp-fire until almost midnight.

At first the Sioux were hostile, but backed down when they saw the team's guns.

Jackrabbit

Prairie dogs

Pronghorn

September 3, 1804

Exploring overland, Lewis sighted strange "goats" which bolted in a flash. They were pronghorn. Only the cheetah runs faster.

More New Species

Also new to science were the jackrabbit (a type of hare) and the prairie dog. Prairie dogs live in warrens with cone-shaped entrances.

September 7, 1804

Prairie dogs dive into their burrows if alarmed. Lewis was keen to get a specimen so he got some of his team to flush one out with water.

October 26, 1804
The team sighted the first Mandan village. Women paddled circular boats made of buffalo hide stretched over a wooden frame. The Mandans were settled farmers, unlike most Plains Indians, who were nomads.

October 26, 1804
The expedition was welcomed by Chief Big White. He was used to foreign visitors. The Mandan villages were the focus of trade between local tribes and also with Canadian fur traders from the north.

BY LATE OCTOBER, with winter closing in, the team was in what is now central North Dakota. The captains were anxious to reach winter quarters at a group of villages belonging to Hidatsa and Mandan tribes, at the furthest point along the Missouri that was known to white traders. There, the expedition was snowed in for five months, but life was made bearable by its friendly Mandan hosts. In spring the keelboat, which was too clumsy to go upriver, was sent home with reports for Jefferson.

The Mandans lived in timber lodges sunk partly into the ground, with thick roofs of earth.

Winter 1804-1805
The Hidatsas, who traveled widely, described the way ahead – a huge waterfall and then the mountains, where the Shoshone people lived.

November 4, 1804
A tough French-Canadian fur trader named Charbonneau came to the fort. He spoke Hidatsa and wanted a job as interpreter on the trip.

November 4, 1804
The captains agreed to take on Charbonneau and one of his two Shoshone wives. He chose 16-year-old Sacagawea, who was expecting a baby.

November 3, 1804
Work began on building the expedition's winter quarters across the river from the village, where there were suitable trees. The captains wanted a strong fort, in case the Sioux Indians attacked.

Winter 1804-1805
The winter was bitterly cold. Men on sentry duty could stand for only half an hour. The frozen Missouri River became a highway for the Mandans' sledges, and for great herds of buffalo.

On New Year's Day the crew danced for the Mandans. Clark's slave, York, was praised most.

December 7, 1804
The Mandans lent the team horses so that they could join in a buffalo hunt in the snow. The Mandans hunted at breakneck speed.

February 5, 1805
Food was getting low and the captains were running out of trade goods. The expedition's blacksmith copied Mandan axes to exchange for maize.

April 7, 1805
The team, now including a mother and baby, set off again, after waving goodbye to the keelboat which returned back east to St Louis.

•THE GREAT FALLS•

May 11, 1805
Precious goods and instruments were almost lost when one of the boats keeled over. The men bailed out water frantically but Sacagawea saved the day – she calmly grabbed objects that were floating away.

May 26, 1805
Lewis climbed to the top of the cliffs that lined the river valley and saw a far-distant range of snow-capped peaks, shining in the sun – the fabled Rocky Mountains were in sight at last!

THE TEAM (now 30 men, plus a mother and baby) in the pirogues and six dugout canoes, were now in unknown territory. Here the plains were home to wolves and grizzly bears. The river ran under cliffs that came to the water's edge. Head winds buffeted the boats, which the team towed through the rocky shallows, their backs burned by the sun, their legs in icy water. In mid-June they reached the waterfalls the Hidatsas had described – not one but five, in 12 miles (20 kilometers) of raging water. The boats had to be transported overland in blistering heat.

On June 13 Lewis escaped from a grizzly bear by swimming into the river. The bear would not swim after him.

June 3, 1805: The river forks
Which was the Missouri? The crew chose the muddy fork. The other fork was clear. The captains chose the clear fork so the crew went this way.

June 7, 1805
Private Windsor slipped on the edge of a 99 foot (30-meter) precipice. Lewis's advice – "cut a foothold with your knife" – saved his life.

June 16, 1805-July 14, 1805
The falls were proof that this was the Missouri River. While Clark went to choose a land route, the men made wheels to transport the boats.

May 1805

Packs of grey wolves were a common sight, lying in wait for a stray buffalo calf or a sick buffalo that could not keep up with the herd. Then the pack of wolves circled its prey and went in for the kill.

May 31, 1805

The river carried the expedition past tall cliffs worn away by wind and rain into all kinds of odd shapes. Some reminded Lewis of towering buildings or classical ruins. Bighorn sheep perched on the rocky pinnacles.

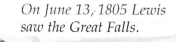

On June 13, 1805 Lewis saw the Great Falls.

Hauling Boats

It took a month to make carriages for the boats and haul them 16.8 miles (28 kilometers) past the falls. In a strong wind the sails helped.

A Freak Storm

The task was made harder by split wheels, bleeding feet, rattlesnakes, grizzly bears, and a freak storm with hailstones as big as apples.

Flash Flood

Sacagawea fell dangerously ill. She was nursed to health by Clark, but then nearly drowned when a flash flood swept down a gully.

•INTO THE ROCKIES•

July 19, 1805
A telltale smoke signal showed that local people were watching but keeping hidden. The smoke meant "Keep clear of the river, alarming strangers sighted!" It was going to be hard to make contact with the locals.

July 21, 1805
Clark led a small party overland to try to meet the invisible watchers. He saw traces of their camps and left presents of cloth as a sign that the Americans had come as friends.

The canoes entered the Rockies through a deep canyon.

BY AUGUST the expedition was high in the Rockies, where the river had shrunk to a stream. Boulders and rapids made canoe travel impossible. But the captains had a plan. The team would shift its gear onto horses, ride over the summit, and make canoes on the far side. The Hidatsas had said the local Shoshones would have horses for sale. But where were the Shoshones? The captains were worried. They must get over the Rockies before it snowed, but without horses they could not get across.

August 1, 1805
The team was near breaking-point from heat, sickness, and dragging the canoes in the swift current, traveling only 3.6 miles (6 kilometers) a day.

August 7, 1805
Spirits rose when Sacagawea recognized a rock on the skyline. It was near her people's summer camp. The Shoshones could not be far off.

August 9, 1805
Moving the boats was becoming impossible. Lewis and three men set off on foot in a desperate bid to find the Shoshones and buy horses.

July 22, 1805
Clark returned with raw, bleeding feet torn by prickly pear, a spiny plant that carpeted the ground. Homemade moccasins were no protection. Clark pulled seventeen spines from one foot.

July 27, 1805: The Three Forks
The mountains opened into a beautiful bowl-shaped plain, ringed with high peaks. Here the river forked into three. The captains took the right-hand fork, toward the western peaks.

Speaking in Hidatsa, so that her husband could translate, Sacagawea told the captains they were camping on the very spot where, five years earlier, Hidatsa raiders had seized her. They had taken her east with them and later sold her to Charbonneau.

August 10, 1805
Lewis's party sighted a Shoshone rider who halted at a distance. As Lewis approached he galloped off, dashing all their hopes.

August 12, 1805
As the party neared the crest of the range, Private MacNeal boasted that he could now bestride the great Missouri River – it was just a trickle.

August 1805
They followed a well-worn trail over a pass. Then they saw what lay ahead – not the hoped-for river plain, but endless mountain peaks.

•THE SHOSHONES•

August 13, 1805

Over the summit, Lewis surprised an old Shoshone woman and a girl, both too scared to move. He gave them gifts, rolled up his shirt to show his white skin, and asked, in signs, to be taken to their chief.

BEYOND THE PASS Lewis met Shoshones. They were friendly, but cautious about selling horses. They had been raided recently by their enemy, the Blackfeet, and feared Lewis was in league with them. Lewis tried to persuade them to return with him to meet the expedition and see that it was genuine.

The Shoshones hung back, suspecting they were being led into an ambush. Lewis tried hinting they were cowards. At last their chief, Cameahwait, decided to go. His trust was rewarded. Among the strangers he found his long lost sister.

August 14, 1805

Lewis asked Chief Cameahwait about the river ahead. The chief drew lines in the sand to represent foaming water, and piled up sand to show rocks overhanging it. He meant boats could not use it.

Lewis was embraced by Chief Cameahwait.

August 17, 1805

Everything about the expedition – boats, guns, the team's appearance – intrigued the Shoshones. Lewis's dog, Seaman, was much admired.

August 18-26, 1805

After making wooden saddles out of paddle blades and boxes, the expedition crossed the pass with Shoshones carrying most of the gear.

August 18-24, 1805

The Shoshones were starving, and even dug up roots to eat. They needed to go east to hunt buffalo. Lewis shamed them into staying to help.

•CROSSING THE PASS•

August 15, 1805
To persuade Cameahwait to help the expedition, Lewis argued that if it succeeded, American traders would soon follow and sell the Shoshones guns. (The Blackfeet already had British guns.)

August 16, 1805
On the journey back to Clark's party the Shoshones, still fearing an ambush, put their fur collars on Lewis and his team, to expose them to being killed as Shoshones. To reassure them Lewis loaned them his guns and hat.

On August 17, Lewis, with the Shoshones, rejoined Clark and the rest of the team and called a conference. When Sacagawea was called in as interpreter she realized suddenly that she knew Chief Cameahwait. He was her brother!

August 24, 1805
Meanwhile Clark had gone ahead to inspect for himself the river below the pass (the Salmon). He was dismayed by what he saw.

August 25-31, 1805
Knowing there was no hope of going ahead by water, the team bargained for horses. Not surprisingly, prices soared.

September 1, 1805
The expedition set off along a mountain trail used by the Nez Perce, a people farther to the west. An elderly Shoshone acted as a guide.

September 3, 1805
The journey was unbelievably difficult. Steep climbs were made worse by huge numbers of fallen trees. The horses skidded and stumbled on stones and fallen timber, and freezing rain turned to snow.

September 10, 1805
Old Toby pointed back to a pass that went well to the north of the one the expedition had used. It was a 5-day journey to the Missouri Falls that way, he said. It had taken the expedition 51 days to make the journey!

THE ROCKIES proved to be not a single range, but many close-packed ranges. Old Toby (as the men named their Shoshone guide) led them along narrow ridges and down steep slopes. In places there was no trail so the guide mistook the way. Horses and team struggled constantly to keep their footing. Supplies were down to a few candles and some bear grease when the explorers at last found a Nez Perce village. Its people led them to the westward-flowing Clearwater River.

Exhausted, hungry and lost in the Bitterroot Mountains.

September 15, 1805
A pack-horse hurtled down 15 feet (40 meters) before its fall was broken by a tree. It survived, but a folding desk belonging to Clark was smashed.

September 18, 1805
Clark and six hunters went on ahead of the main team to seek game lower down. Snow hid the trail and crashed down from branches.

September 20, 1805
While the baggage team struggled on behind, Clark's party got clear of the forest and was taken in and fed by Nez Perce villagers.

• A REAL CRISIS •

September 12, 1805
After following a long ridge northwards, Old Toby began to lead the expedition west into more mountains (the Bitterroot range). They passed hot springs, where near-boiling water spouted from rocks.

September 14, 1805
By now food stocks were nearly finished and the expedition's hunters returned empty-handed. They could find no game to shoot so high in the mountains. A horse had to be killed to provide supper.

On September 17, the team had a crisis talk. Should they give up or go on, and was there a choice? The team was too weak to go back the way it had come.

Branding iron ——

September 22-30, 1805
Lewis's team staggered into the Nez Perce village too. Then the whole expedition collapsed sick, unable to leave the camp for a week.

October 1-6, 1805
Nez Perce chief Twisted Hair helped Clark find large trees to make canoes, and showed him how to hollow them out over a slow-burning fire.

October 17, 1805
The horses were marked with a branding iron and left with Chief Twisted Hair. The team took to boats again to continue their journey.

October 8-13, 1805

The boats sailed through swirling rapids, often 15 in a day. The clumsy canoes got swamped, overturned, sprang leaks, and goods were washed away. But the current was speeding the expedition west at last!

October 18-13, 1805

The Snake and Columbia rivers were full of salmon. It was the basic food of the Nez Perce tribes whose villages lined the banks. The explorers lived on dried salmon until they hated it.

Shooting rapids at The Dalles on the Columbia River.

OVERJOYED to be on the river again, the captains were keen to keep moving at all costs. The Clearwater was a swift mountain river, full of rapids which the team shot recklessly. The canoes were swept into the powerful Snake River that flowed west through deep canyons. On October 18, the team at last entered the Columbia River. It was very dangerous, but after shooting fearsome rapids, to the amazement of Chinook onlookers, the triumphant explorers reached the Pacific coast.

November 3, 1805

The team got their first hint of the sea! Beyond a tall rock (Beacon Rock), the expedition noticed the river starting to rise and fall like a tide.

November 4, 1805

Villagers wearing European-style jackets, shirts, and hats had clearly been trading with the British. The sea must be close.

November 5, 1805

The expedition met seacoast Chinooks in highly carved and painted canoes. These impressed Clark so much he made a sketch of them.

October 8-13, 1805
The team longed for meat, but there was nothing to shoot along the Snake River. The Nez Perce sold them dog meat. Some of them even liked it, but Clark could never bear the taste.

October 24, 1805
The canoes were lowered by rope through the Celilo Falls.

The captains visited a Chinook chief's lodge.

November 7, 1805: Thick Fog
After a miserable, wet night camped on a small patch of stones the team woke to dense fog. The boats could not set off until it cleared.

The Sea At Last
As the sun came out the team suddenly raised a shout – "the sea!" They heard waves breaking on rocks and could see it far away.

Triumph
That night, in a rain-sodden camp, Clark wrote in triumph in his journal "Ocian 4142 Miles from the Mouth of Missouri R."

•ON THE PACIFIC•

November 10-15, 1805
The expedition camped on the north side of the estuary. The weather was terrible – gales and endless rain. Giant waves drove fallen trees against the camp and made travel impossible.

November 16, 1805
Lewis explored the north shore of the estuary. Where it met the sea he carved his name on a tree. He then went some way along the coast, looking for trading ships, but the coastline was deserted.

AFTER WEEKS camped on the Columbia estuary, the team found a sheltered spot for a winter home. It was named Fort Clatsop after the local tribe. The Clatsops were friendly and willing to sell food, but the team was very short of goods to trade. The captains had hoped to find an American ship that would carry everyone home, or a trading post where they could buy goods on credit. There was no sign of either. It was plain that they would have to return the way they had come.

The Clatsops were regular visitors to the fort. They sold food, but were not trusted in the fort at night.

December 7-24, 1805
They voted to camp on the south side of the estuary. Working in constant rain, the team cut down trees and split logs to build a fort.

December 25, 1805
Christmas dinner was rotting elk meat, stale pounded fish and a few roots. Gifts were exchanged. Sacagawea gave Clark 24 weasel tails.

January-February 1806
Five men were sent to camp on the coast, to boil sea water to make salt which everyone was craving. Others made new clothes from elk hide.

Sea otter

November 18, 1805
Sacagawea had to part with her blue bead belt, because the captains badly wanted a beautiful sea-otter robe and that was the price demanded. They gave her a coat instead.

November 24, 1805
The team voted on where to pass the winter – at the present wet camp, back at the falls, or on the other bank. Everyone had a vote. Sacagawea said she wanted a spot where there were plenty of edible roots.

In January a whale was found on shore but the Clatsops had stripped it of blubber by the time Clark's team arrived.

January-March 1806
Clark wrote up his journals, including sketches (*above*) of wildlife and the Chinook custom of shaping babies' heads in a special cradle.

January-March 1806
The captains shared the task of record keeping. Their journals, describing in every detail all they had seen, were their most precious cargo.

March 23, 1806
The team loaded their canoes and said goodbye to Fort Clatsop. They were on their way home at last!

• A HEROES' WELCOME •

July 4, 1806

Lewis's party used the pass Old Toby had pointed out the previous year. The Nez Perce guides said anxious goodbyes. They had become the team's friends and warned that dangerous Blackfoot territory was ahead.

July 22, 1806

Lewis turned back disappointed. He had hoped the muddy Marias River rose in the north, in areas claimed by the British, in which case these would be part of Louisiana. But the river veered west into the Rockies.

B Y MAY the team had collected its horses from the Nez Perce, re-entered the mountains and found the trail snow-blocked. The party was rescued and guided by some Nez Perce. It then split up to inspect new routes. Lewis explored the muddy river seen the previous June. There he had the expedition's only serious clash with Native Americans. Clark went via the Three Forks, then down the Yellowstone River to the Missouri where the teams met again. Two months later they returned to St. Louis to a heroes' welcome.

On July 26, Lewis, with only three men, encountered eight Blackfoot warriors.

July 10, 1806

Meanwhile Sacagawea, who was now in her homeland again, guided Clark's party from the Three Forks to the Yellowstone River.

July 20, 1806

Clark's team went at top speed down the Yellowstone on a craft made of two huge tree trunks supporting a raft large enough to carry them all.

August 12, 1806

When Lewis's party rejoined Clark's on the Missouri, Clark was alarmed to find Lewis lying on his stomach in the bottom of his boat.

July 27, 1806
After a tense discussion with the Blackfeet both sides camped together. At dawn the Blackfeet tried to steal the rifles. There was a scuffle in which a Blackfoot was fatally stabbed by one of Lewis's men.

July 27, 1806
The Blackfeet tried to run off with the horses. Lewis warned he would shoot, then fired, hitting one. They all fled. Fearing a revenge attack from the whole tribe, Lewis's party rode hard all day and into the night.

On September 23, most of St. Louis turned out to meet the heroes.

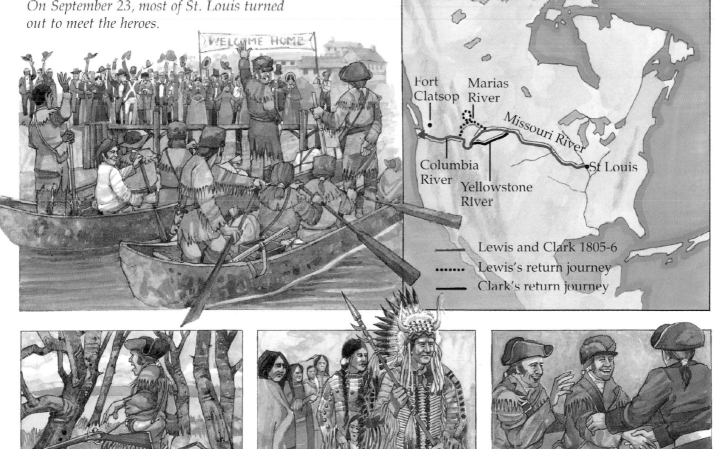

WELCOME HOME

Fort Clatsop
Marias River
Missouri River
Columbia River
Yellowstone River
St Louis

——— Lewis and Clark 1805-6
········ Lewis's return journey
——— Clark's return journey

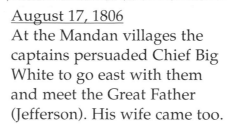

August 12, 1806
Lewis explained that they had been stalking elk. One of the men heard a rustling in the trees, fired, and shot his captain in the behind!

August 17, 1806
At the Mandan villages the captains persuaded Chief Big White to go east with them and meet the Great Father (Jefferson). His wife came too.

September 17, 1806
An old friend of Lewis's, traveling upriver to trade, greeted the team in amazement. "Everyone thinks you're dead," he cried.

LEWIS AND CLARK had fulfilled almost all of Jefferson's hopes. They had mapped the way to the Pacific and had made many new scientific discoveries. But their news was not all good. The easy waterway that Jefferson had pictured did not exist: instead they had found "tremendous mountains which for 60 miles are covered in eternal snows." But they had other, better news that sent fur trappers rushing west to make their fortunes along the Missouri; there were rivers with more beaver "than any other streams on earth."

THE FIRST ATTEMPT at a transcontinental fur empire, funded by John Jacob Astor in 1810, was a disaster. The distances were too great and the way too hard. Some people starved on the journey, others drowned. But the trappers were not discouraged. Many took to living and hunting out in the Louisiana wilds.

SINCE HOSTILE Blackfeet kept trappers away from the upper Missouri they looked for routes farther south and discovered better ways across the mountains. In 1824 trapper Jedediah Smith found South Pass, in present-day Wyoming, a relatively easy passage over the Rockies. In time it became known as the gateway to the west. By the 1830s speculators were going overland, via South Pass, to set up west-coast businesses. They were followed by missionaries who wanted to convert the Native Americans to Christianity. In the 1840s people began packing their belongings into wagons and trekking over the mountains to start a new life in the west. Jefferson's dream of one nation from coast to coast became a reality.

AND WHAT became of the expedition's members? Lewis was made governor of the Louisiana Territory and Clark its Superintendent of Indian Affairs. The enlisted members of the team were given grants of land. Clark's slave, York, who was not one of these but had done as much as anyone on the trip, asked Clark to grant him his freedom as a reward.

Even though Clark was a kind and generous man by early 19th-century standards, he thought this was an unreasonable demand and refused.

CHIEF BIG WHITE visited Washington and was escorted back to his people in 1809. Sacagawea and her husband remained with the Mandans. Clark had grown very fond of Sacagawea's little son (nicknamed Pompey) and offered to adopt him. His mother was unwilling to part with him at first, but when he was old enough she allowed him to be taken east and educated at Clark's expense.

CLARK lived to a contented old age, but Lewis had a tragic end. He was vulnerable to depression, mismanaged his finances, and shot himself in 1809 at the age of 35.

Blackfeet
A Plains-Indian tribe of the upper Missouri, greatly feared for its ferocious treatment of its neighbors.

Blubber
The fat of a whale.

Branding iron
A red-hot piece of metal used to mark livestock, as proof of ownership.

Buffalo (properly called bison)
Very large wild cattle. Enormous herds lived on the North American Plains until the mid-19th century, when white settlers shot almost all of them.

Chinooks
A salmon-fishing and hunting people of the lower Columbia River.

Clatsops
A tribe of the Chinook nation.

Court martial
A trial by a military court.

Coyote
A scavenging animal of the dog family.

The Dalles
A point on the Columbia River where huge rocks caused mighty rapids.

Estuary
The mouth of a river, where tidal waters meet the river's current.

Hidatsas
Plains-Indian allies of the Mandans.

Keelboat
A long, barge-like riverboat, used on the Mississippi and Missouri rivers for shipping goods.

Mandans
Plains Indians of the upper Missouri who lived in villages, and who hunted buffalo as well as farmed the land.

Moccasins
Flat shoes made of animal skin, in a Native-American style.

Nez Perce
(From the French for "pierced nose" though they did not pierce their noses). A people of the plateau land west of the Rockies.

Nomads
Peoples whose way of life makes it necessary for them to move from place to place in order to farm or hunt.

Otoes
Plains Indians of the lower Missouri.

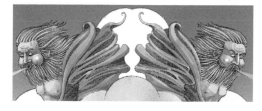

Pirogue
An open boat, with or without a sail.

Plains Indians
Native American peoples of the Great Plains (the vast grasslands of central North America).

Prairies
Rich, lush grasslands of the lower Missouri.

Shoshones
A large group of peoples living west of the Rockies as hunter-gatherers. When horse ownership spread (from the Spanish) among Native Americans, some Shoshone tribes rode seasonally to the Great Plains, to hunt buffalo.

Sioux
The dominant Plains Indians of the lower Missouri. They were fierce warriors and enemies of the Mandans and Hidatsas.

INDEX

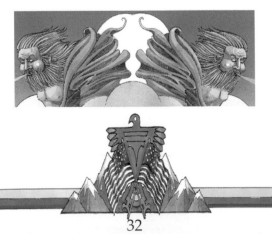